PUZZLE OCEAN

Susannah Leigh

Illustrated by Brenda Haw

Contents

Series Editor: Gaby Waters
Assistant Editor: Michelle Bates

About this book

This book is about a girl named Rosie and her amazing adventure in the underwater world of Puzzle Ocean. There are puzzles to solve on every double page. If you get stuck, you can look at the answers on pages 31 and 32.

Rosie

The seaside

Rosie's adventure begins one Sunday afternoon at the seaside. Whenever Rosie visits the seaside she plays with her friend Milly. There is something very special about Milly which you will find out later on.

All sorts of fantastic things lie at the bottom of Puzzle Ocean. There's even a pirate ship called the Jolly Dodger. Once there was treasure on board the Jolly Dodger. Now the treasure is scattered across the ocean floor.

JOLLY DODGER

Things to spot

Rosie's friend Milly collects the Jolly Dodger pirate treasure as they go. There is a piece of treasure on every double page. Can you collect it too? It might be useful later on. Here are the things to look out for.

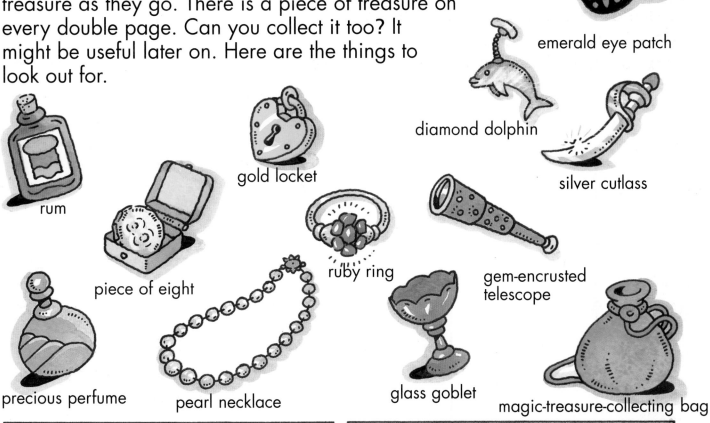

emerald eye patch

diamond dolphin

silver cutlass

gold locket

rum

piece of eight

ruby ring

gem-encrusted telescope

precious perfume

pearl necklace

glass goblet

magic-treasure-collecting bag

Yellow-clawed lobsters
Beware of the yellow-clawed lobsters! They like pinching things. Can you spot a yellow-clawed lobster on every double page? The lobsters have a sneaky friend called Jasper. You will meet him later on.

Blue oysters
Puzzle Ocean is home to the rare blue ocean oysters. There is at least one blue oyster hiding shyly on each double page. See if you can find them all.

3

On the beach

On Sunday afternoon, Rosie was paddling in the ocean. Suddenly she saw a bottle bobbing in the water. Rosie picked it up. Inside was a message. What's more, it was for her! But Rosie wasn't surprised. It was from her friend Milly. Milly always sent Rosie a message in a bottle when she wanted to play. But as Rosie read the note, she gasped. It said there was trouble in Puzzle Ocean! She had to find Milly.

Where is Milly? Can you see what is special about her?

Ocean trouble

Rosie rushed over to the blue rock pool. Sure enough, her friend Milly the mermaid was waiting.

"Something dreadful has happened in Puzzle Ocean, Rosie," Milly said. "We need some human help."

Milly began to explain ...

Someone has stolen the King of Puzzle Ocean's golden crown!

Ah ha. Now I will be king. xxx J

King's Golden Crown

Whoever holds the crown for a day and a night will become King of Puzzle Ocean.

The crown has been gone for hours. If we don't hurry, the thief will become King.

I'm sure the thief is nasty merman Jasper and his sneaky lobster friends. They're always pinching things.

"Look Rosie. There's Jasper now,"
Milly cried. "And he's got the crown."

Can you see Jasper?

7

Milly's plan

Jasper dived beneath the waves with the golden crown and disappeared.

"Quick Rosie, we must follow Jasper and get the crown back," said Milly. "Come with me and I'll explain how you can help."

She took Rosie to a cave away from the busy beach and began to tell her what she had to do ...

"Jasper must be taking the crown to his Puzzle Ocean home," Milly said. "It has a secret entrance, but we'll never find that in time. The only other way in is over a sand bank. I can't walk across the sand bank with my fishy tail, but you could Rosie. Will you help?"

"Of course I will, Milly," Rosie said bravely.

"Thank you," Milly cried. "First we will have to journey deep into Puzzle Ocean to find Jasper's home. I'll make something magic to help you breathe underwater. I need some red seaweed, a blue pebble, a yellow pebble, a green starfish and two green flippers. Can you help me, Rosie?"

Can you find everything?

Underwater

Rosie found everything. Milly said some magic mermaid words. In a flash, Rosie was holding a shimmery cobweb.

"Slip this under your top, Rosie," Milly said. "It will help you breathe like a fish. The flippers are for your feet."

Milly took Rosie's hand as they dived beneath the waves.

This was the first time Rosie had been under the water. She could breathe but swimming wasn't so easy. Suddenly she bumped into an octopus. It squirted a cloud of green ink and scared all the sea creatures. When the ink cleared, several things had changed – and Milly had vanished.

Can you spot the differences? Where is Milly?

A fishy problem

Rosie helped Milly out from behind the chest where she was looking at a scrap of paper. The chest was empty, except for one piece of treasure which they picked up. They put it in their bag and paddled on. Before long they found themselves at St. Fisher's school.

"Naughty Jasper passed by earlier and caused a terrible commotion," wailed Mrs. Mullet, the teacher. "Now these little fishes are being naughty too. Some are in the wrong classes and some are hiding. Can you help me sort them out? There should be six rainbow fish in the art class, five orange clowny fish in the juggling class, four blue stickybacks in the music class and seven green goober fish in the sports class."

Can you find all the fish and send them to the right classes?

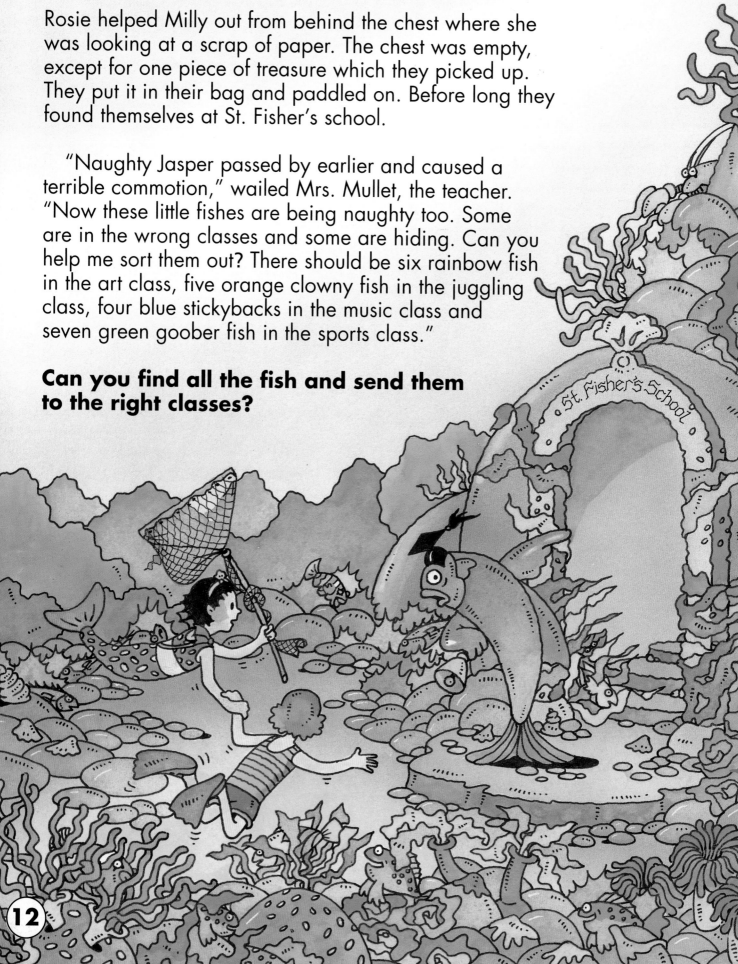

MUSIC CLASS

four stickybacks

JUGGLING CLASS

five clowny fish

SPORTS CLASS

seven goober fish

ART CLASS

six rainbow fish

Overboard!

Soon all the naughty fish were in the right classes. Mrs. Mullet was very pleased.

Rosie and Milly swam on. Up above, shapes moved on the water.

"Fishing boats!" Rosie said.

"Look," said Milly. "They have caught some very strange objects. I wonder if Jasper is responsible for this tangle of trouble."

"Listen Milly," Rosie said. "Everyone thinks they have caught very big fish!"

Can you untangle all the ropes and see what each boat has really caught?

Shell searching

Milly and Rosie untangled the last of the ropes and the two friends headed on toward Jasper's lair. All the while they kept a lookout for some of Jasper's mischief.

They soon found it. A small group of underwater creatures huddled together looking very cold.

"Oh Milly," they cried. "Jasper has frightened us all out of our shells – and hidden them too. Can you help us find them? Our shells match our bodies."

Can you find all the lost shells?

Sharks!

The sea creatures wriggled back into their shells. Milly and Rosie waved goodbye.

"Jasper's probably home by now," Milly said. "We must get the crown back. If Jasper becomes King, Puzzle Ocean will be a terrible place to live."

They kept an eye out for Jasper.

They dived deep down ...

... and up to the surface.

They swam with friendly dolphins.

Suddenly they saw large creatures circling around them. Sharks!

"The only thing Puzzle Ocean sharks like chomping better than mer-people are seaweed sandwiches," cried Milly. "Quick, Rosie! There are sure to be some lying around."

Can you find each shark a seaweed sandwich?

Spiky sand bank

The sharks swallowed the seaweed sandwiches and swam away. Milly and Rosie journeyed on to shallower water. Suddenly, ahead of them loomed the sand bank. Beyond it lay Jasper's lair. Rosie shivered. Now she was on her own …

"Head for the pink glow in the sky, Rosie," said Milly. "But be careful. The bank is made of squelchy sand. If you step in it you'll sink!"

Can you find a safe route across the sand bank to the pink glow?

SQUELCHY
SAND

A shadowy cave

Rosie scrambled safely to the other side of the sand bank. Here, the sand dipped away to the sea again. Rosie dived beneath the waves. She didn't have to swim long before she reached a shadowy cave. Was this where Jasper lived?

Cautiously she peered inside. There was no sign of him, but Rosie saw several things which made her think it really was Jasper's cave. And then she spotted something which made her certain.

Could this be Jasper's cave?
What has Rosie spotted?

LOBSTER SLIPPERS

FLIPPER SLIPPER

Rescue Rosie

There was no sign of Jasper. Quickly, Rosie lifted the golden crown down from its hiding place. But suddenly she heard a noise behind her. She turned around and found herself face to face with Jasper and his lobster pals!

"Ah ha! An intruder," Jasper smirked. "You're in trouble. I'm going to make you my prisoner!"

With that he lunged forward to grab Rosie and the crown. Was this the end for Rosie? Would she be trapped in Jasper's cave forever?

What do you think?

Milly's bargain

Silently, Milly scuttled up on the back of a spotted crab. She threw a big net over Jasper and the lobsters, and they were caught before they knew it!

"This friendly sea creature gave me a lift across the sand bank," Milly smiled.

"You'll never get away with this!" Jasper cackled.

Rosie clutched the crown.

But the lobsters cut through the net!

Milly remembered something ...

I've got lots more amazing treasure, Jasper. You can have it all if you let us take the crown.

Hmm. Lots of treasure? Yes please!

Oh no.

But ...

... Milly's treasure was gone!

Do you know what Milly's treasure is? Can you find it here?

Fishy feast

Jasper and the lobsters were very happy with the pirate treasure. They were so busy trying it on that they didn't see Rosie and Milly sneak away with the golden crown.

The friendly crab gave Milly and Rosie a piggyback over the sand bank. Then the two friends swam on to the King of Puzzle Ocean's castle.

That evening, the King held a great feast to celebrate, and awarded Milly and Rosie special shell medals for being so brave. Rosie and Milly were very happy and danced with all their ocean friends.

How many ocean friends do you recognize at the party?

Goodbye

After the feast it was time for Rosie to go.

"Keep your shimmery cobweb, Rosie," said Milly. "You never know when you might need it again."

"Thank you, Milly," said Rosie. "But there's one thing I don't understand …"

"…Why did you give the precious pirate treasure to Jasper?"

"The treasure wasn't so precious," Milly smiled. "Don't you remember the chest and the scrap of paper inside it?"

What did the paper say? (Look back at page 11.)

Answers

Pages 4-5
On the beach

Milly is here.

Milly is a mermaid!

Pages 6-7
Ocean trouble

Jasper is here.

Pages 8-9
Milly's plan

The things Milly needs are circled in black.

Pages 10-11
Underwater!

The differences are circled in black.

Milly is here.

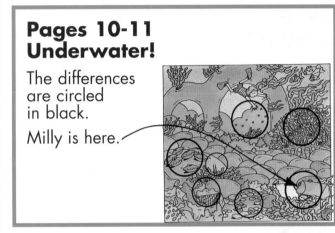

Pages 12-13
A fishy problem

The fish for the music class are circled in black. The fish for the juggling class are circled in red. The fish for the sports class are circled in blue. The fish for the art class are circled in yellow.

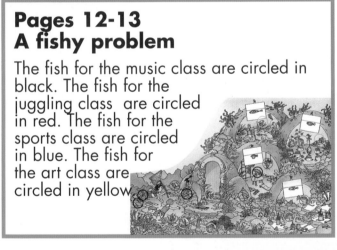

Pages 14-15
Overboard!

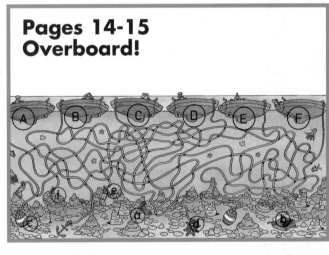

Pages 16-17
Shell searching

The lost shells are circled in black.

Pages 18-19
Sharks!

The seaweed sandwiches are circled in black.

Pages 20-21
Spiky sand bank

The safe route is shown in black.

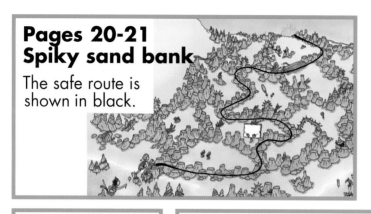

Pages 22-23
A shadowy cave

Rosie has spotted the golden crown. The things that make Rosie think this is Jasper's cave are circled in black.

Pages 24-25
Rescue Rosie!

Rosie has spotted Milly coming to her rescue.

Pages 26-27
Milly's bargain

Milly wants to give Jasper the Jolly Dodger treasure she picked up on the way. Here it is, all collected in the magic-treasure-collecting bag.

Pages 28-29
Fishy feast

Look back through the book and see how many faces you recognize here.

Page 30
Goodbye

The paper said that the Jolly Dodger treasure was fake. This means it is not worth anything.

Did you spot everything?
Blue oysters

Jolly Dodger Treasure

Yellow-clawed lobsters

The chart below shows you how many blue oysters are hiding on each double page. You can also find out which piece of Jolly Dodger treasure is hidden where.

Did you remember to look out for Jasper's sneaky yellow-clawed lobster pals? Look back through the book again and see if you can spot them.

Pages	Blue oysters	Jolly Dodger treasure
4-5	three	magic-treasure-collecting bag
6-7	two	silver cutlass
8-9	three	precious perfume
10-11	one	pearl necklace
12-13	four	rum
14-15	three	gold locket
16-17	two	piece of eight
18-19	two	ruby ring
20-21	two	emerald eye patch
22-23	four	diamond dolphin
24-25	one	glass goblet
26-27	three	gem-encrusted telescope
28-29	three	all of the treasure is here!

This edition first published in 2003 by Usborne Publishing Ltd., Usborne House, 83-85 Saffron Hill, London EC1N 8RT, England.

www.usborne.com Copyright © 2003, 1996 Usborne Publishing Ltd.

First published in America August 1996.